RAINTREE BIOGRAPHIES

George Washington

Mary Stout

RAINTREE
STECK-VAUGHN
PUBLISHERS

A Harcourt Company

Austin   New York
www.raintreesteckvaughn.com

Published by Raintree Steck-Vaughn Publishers, an imprint of Steck-Vaughn Company.

Project Editors: Sean Dolan, Leigh Ann Cobb, Rebecca Hunter
Production Manager: Richard Johnson
Designed by Ian Winton

Planned and produced by Discovery Books

Library of Congress Cataloging-in-Publication Data
Available upon request.

ISBN 0-7398-5681-2

Printed and bound in China
1 2 3 4 5 6 7 8 9 0 07 06 05 04 03 02

Acknowledgments
The publishers would like to thank the following for permission to reproduce their pictures:
Cover: The Bridgeman Art Library; pages 4, 5, 6, 7, 8, 9, Peter Newark's American Pictures; pages 10, 11, The Bridgeman
Art Library; pages 12, 13, Peter Newark's American Pictures; page 14, The Bridgeman Art Library; page 15, The Granger
Collection; pages 16, 17, 18, 20, Peter Newark's American Pictures; page 21, Corbis; pages 22, 23, Peter Newark's
American Pictures; page 24, The Bridgeman Art Library; pages 25, 26, 27, 28, 29, Peter Newark's American Pictures.

CONTENTS

THE FIRST PRESIDENT

George Washington was at home on April 14, 1789, when he got the news. He had been elected to be the very first president of the United States! He packed and left his home, Mount Vernon, two days later to travel to the temporary capital of the United States, New York City.

George Washington was America's first commander-in-chief, so he had to make up his own uniform. He worked with a tailor to create the tan and blue uniforms he wore during the Revolutionary War against the British.

George Washington knew that the job of president would be a difficult one. No one had ever done it before. He was worried whether he would do it well. He wanted to travel quietly and think about his future position. But the people of the United States were happy that Washington was president. At every town he traveled through, people cheered and church bells rang. A special barge was even built, decorated in red, white, and blue, to transport him across the Hudson River to New York City.

Washington takes the 35-word oath of office. Provided in the Constitution, the oath is the only part of the inauguration ceremony required by law. However, Washington added "so help me God" at the end of his oath, and so has almost every president after him.

Inauguration Day was April 30, 1789. President Washington's inauguration took place at the Federal Hall. He stood on the balcony clad in a brown suit, made in America, white stockings, and carrying a sword. After the ceremony, Washington gave a speech and went to church. That night, there was a huge party. Washington the general had just become Washington the president. He was the only elected head of government in the world.

YOUNG GEORGE

George Washington was born on February 22, 1732, at Wakefield farm in the Virginia colony. At this time, Virginia was one of 13 British colonies along the eastern coast of North America. These colonies were governed by Great Britain but were not separately represented in the British parliament.

Wakefield was the plantation where George Washington was born. It was located in Virginia, on the Rappahannock River.

George's father was a tobacco farmer, and George had six brothers and sisters. His favorite was his older brother Lawrence, who was affectionate and wise. George grew up wanting to be just like him. Lawrence was an officer in the local militia. When their father died, Lawrence inherited Mount Vernon, another family property, and George went to live with him there. His brother encouraged George to ride horses, meet people, and dance. He also made sure he studied hard, because there was no money to send him to school in England, where Lawrence had been educated.

George was good at math. He used his grandfather's surveying tools to measure and map out Lawrence's turnip field when he was 15 years old. Pretty soon he was surveying land for friends and neighbors to earn money. By the time he was 17, George had important jobs surveying land in the wilderness. He had to travel a long way, camp out, and hunt. He had to map and measure land where no white man had ever gone before.

Washington got his first taste of "roughing it" on surveying expeditions. Once, he was bitten by lice, his tent constantly blew down, and the straw on which he slept even caught fire!

GEORGE LEGENDS

The famous story about Washington being too honest to lie to his father about chopping down his cherry tree is just a legend. Americans told many such legends about Washington. They show how highly his countrymen thought of him.

THE FRENCH AND INDIAN WAR

In 1751 George accompanied Lawrence to Barbados, where Lawrence went for his tuberculosis. Lawrence died the following year. George had to decide what he would do with his life. At 20 years old, he decided to join the militia.

George took Lawrence's place as a major in the Virginia colony's militia. Virginia's governor, Robert Dinwiddie, sent George on a dangerous mission to the Ohio territory. He was to warn the French not to build forts, since the land was claimed by the British.

Lawrence went to the Caribbean island of Barbados because the climate there was supposed to be good for respiratory illnesses. This was the only time George ever left the 13 colonies or the United States.

However, the French insisted that they owned the Ohio territory. When George gave his message, the French refused to obey and said that they would fight for the territory. George traveled through a terrible blizzard to bring this news back to the governor.

The governor sent Washington, now promoted to Lieutenant Colonel, back with 300 men to attack the French post at Fort Duquesne. They attacked a group of French soldiers on the way to the fort. Then 900 French and Native Americans found and attacked Washington's men, and he surrendered. This battle started what is now called the French and Indian War.

When the British army came to fight in the French and Indian War, Washington went with them to help. There were many arguments between the Virginia militia and the British military over the best way to fight in the American wilderness. Washington observed the British military to obtain formal military training. This knowledge was to help him later.

George Washington was an aide to the British general Edward Braddock during the French and Indian War. During a fierce battle, Washington's hat was shot off his head, and his horse was killed. Washington lived, but Braddock was badly wounded and later died.

In 1755 Governor Dinwiddie made Washington commander of the entire Virginia militia. His job was to build 81 small forts to guard the frontier against raids by Native Americans. By 1758, however, George had decided to resign from the army. He was frustrated by army life and being denied the payment for his services he felt he deserved. He returned to Mount Vernon to become a farmer.

George the Farmer

At 27 years old, George Washington was tall and slender, with reddish-brown hair and gray-blue eyes. In Virginia he was thought of as a war hero. He was, however, shy and awkward with women. No one is sure how he met Martha Dandridge Custis, but in 1759 they got married at her home. She was a very rich widow with two young children. Martha was about the same age as George, and was short with brown hair and hazel eyes. She was plump, cheerful, and friendly, where George was quiet and serious. They were unable to have children together, but George adopted Patsy and Jacky, Martha's children from her first husband.

This picture of George and Martha's wedding was painted by Jean Leon Jerome Ferris. Martha wore a white wedding dress made of silk and satin. Martha's children, Patsy, age 2, and Jacky, age 4, were also at the wedding.

GEORGE WASHINGTON'S TEETH

Many think that George Washington had wooden teeth, but this is another legend. It is true that he had false teeth because he lost most of his teeth or had them pulled out. He had several pairs of false teeth. One set was carved from a hippopotamus tusk. All of them were heavy and did not fit very well. This made it difficult for George to speak. It also made him unwilling to smile.

Washington became a member of the House of Burgesses, which was the Virginia colony's legislature. With Martha's property and Mount Vernon, the plantation that he inherited from his brother, George was a rich man. He finally had the kind of life that he had always wanted: running a farm, having a family, and meeting with the Virginia Legislature.

Washington said about life on his plantation, "I had rather be at home at Mount Vernon with a friend or two about me, than to be attended at the seat of the government by the officers of State and the representatives of every power in Europe."

PLANTATION LIFE

George Washington got up early each day. In his office, he read the newspapers, wrote letters, and noted expenses in his account books. After eating breakfast with his family, he saddled a horse to ride over his five farms. Most plantations grew only tobacco, but George knew that it was smart to plant other crops. So he grew corn, wheat, and oats, and also raised animals for food. After tending to his farms and solving any problems, he returned to the house at 2 o'clock to eat dinner. This might be roast pork, vegetables, and pudding. George and Martha liked to entertain neighbors and friends. He also loved fox-hunting.

Here, Washington enjoys one of his favorite sports, fox-hunting, with a few friends. Fellow Virginian and rebel Thomas Jefferson said that Washington was "the best horseman of his age."

Hundreds of slaves lived and worked at Mount Vernon. They did such jobs as planting, tending, and harvesting crops; grinding wheat; making shoes for people and horses; tending to livestock; and cooking and cleaning in the main house.

Mount Vernon was a very large plantation. It took much skilled and manual labor to maintain the five farms and big house there. Washington's family had always owned slaves, and he depended on their work. Mount Vernon had over 300 slaves when Washington died. He often commented privately that he thought slavery should be stopped, but publicly he did not take a stand. He kept his slaves until he died, but on his death they were freed.

Abolishing Slavery

"…It being among my first wishes to see some plan adopted by the legislature, by which slavery in this country may be abolished…."

Letter from George Washington to John Francis Mercer, September 9, 1786

13

Washington Becomes a Rebel

Until this time, Washington was content for the British to rule over the American colonies. His grandfather came from England, and Washington probably considered himself English to a degree. But Great Britain needed money. Its war with France was expensive. King George III of Britain decided to obtain money by taxing some of the British goods sent to the American colonies. The Stamp Act required colonists to buy a stamp that had to be put on most kinds of printed material, including newspapers and books.

Other taxes were put on products such as sugar, glass, and tea. These extra taxes made everything cost more, and this made Americans angry. The legislatures of the different colonies began writing letters to each other. They shared how they felt and suggested actions they could take together. Twelve of the thirteen colonies sent representatives to meet in Philadelphia in 1774.

Colonists in Boston in 1765 protested the Stamp Act by rioting and torching buildings.

Delegates from all the colonies met in Philadelphia in September 1774 for the First Continental Congress.

This meeting was called the First Continental Congress. The Virginia colony sent George Washington to the Continental Congress. Washington didn't say very much at the Congress, but he wore his military uniform to the meetings. He was the only one there who had fought in a war. Though he had never won a battle, he was reliable and respected.

The Second Continental Congress met again in Philadelphia in 1775. The Congress decided the colonies needed a combined army alongside their state militias. The Congress elected George Washington to be general and commander-in-chief of the Continental Army. George agreed to lead the troops against the British army. He became a rebel in what was to become the Revolutionary War.

A Daunting Task

"… I declare with the utmost sincerity, I do not think myself equal to the command I am honored with."

Washington's address to the Second Continental Congress, June 15, 1775

THE REVOLUTIONARY WAR

Washington traveled north to Massachusetts in July 1775 to lead the Continental army. He was shocked to find 15,000 men with no training and no uniforms. They were all volunteers, and they brought their own guns. Much work had to be done, to supply them and train them to fight.

Washington's Army

"Are these the men with whom I am to defend America?"

Washington after his first review of the Continental army

Washington had to make good soldiers out of a group of volunteers from different states. At first, his new soldiers had no uniforms, very little food, and weren't paid when they were promised.

Washington's men first forced the British out of Boston, Massachusetts. Then, they turned their attention to the colony of New York. George was in New York with his troops on July 4, 1776, when the Declaration of Independence was signed in Philadelphia. This declared that the American colonies were no longer a part of Britain.

SOLDIER'S PAY

Their new country had no money, so the first volunteers for the Continental army did not get paid. On December 31, 1776, the Continental Congress voted to give $20 and 100 acres of land to every soldier that signed up to be in the army until the war was over. But they would not receive this until long after the war.

Washington's army was not able to win New York City from the British. The British army chased them out of New York, through New Jersey, and into Pennsylvania. Many battles took place, and the Continental army barely managed to avoid destruction.

The American Declaration of Independence was signed by the men in the Continental Congress in Philadelphia, Pennsylvania, on July 4, 1776. George Washington is not in the picture, since he was in New York leading the American troops in battle.

CHRISTMAS DAY VICTORY

In early December 1776, Washington and his army retreated across the Delaware River to Pennsylvania. By now, Washington had less than half the troops that he had when the campaign began. Many men had quit because of hunger and sickness. The new troops that were expected did not arrive. Washington was greatly worried.

On Christmas night, Washington led 2,400 troops across the Delaware River to launch a surprise attack on the British. A horrible snowstorm delayed the crossing of Washington's men, their horses, and 18 cannon in old boats and rafts. By dawn, however, they were marching toward Trenton, New Jersey.

> *"It will be a terrible night for those who have no shoes. Some of them have tied only rags about their feet: others are barefoot, but I have not heard a man complain."* So wrote Colonel John Fitzgerald, as the American troops started to cross the icy Delaware.

A few days after the American troops surprised the British with a Christmas Day attack, they met again in Princeton, New Jersey. The Americans won the Battle of Princeton and chased the British troops out of New Jersey.

Sleepy and unprepared after spending the day celebrating Christmas, the British forces were not expecting an attack. The Americans quickly overwhelmed them, killing 100 and taking 1,000 as prisoners. No Americans were killed. Victory at the Battle of Trenton gave the American people reason to believe they might actually win the war.

Even so, by 1777 the Continental army had shrunk to only 1,600 men. Fortunately for Washington, reinforcements arrived from Pennsylvania bringing the total to just over 5,000. When Washington offered to pay their salaries out of his own pocket, 1,300 Continental soldiers agreed to stay on.

THE TURNING POINT IN THE WAR

In 1777 the British developed a plan to defeat the American rebels. A force led by General John Burgoyne was to march southward from Canada and join with troops led by Sir William Howe that were marching northward from New York City.

Burgoyne's troops began their move southward. But instead of going north, Howe took his men into Pennsylvania. Burgoyne's forces found themselves surrounded by a larger American force and surrendered after being defeated at the Battle of Saratoga in upstate New York.

THE MARQUIS DE LAFAYETTE

The Marquis de Lafayette was a young nobleman from France who believed in the Americans' cause. He wanted to help them fight the British. When he was only 19 years old, he sailed to America. He joined the American Army and became very good friends with George Washington. Washington loved Lafayette like a son. In the Battle of Brandywine, Lafayette fought bravely and was wounded with a bullet in his leg. He helped the Americans until the war was over, then he sailed back to France to live with his wife and children.

The American victory at Saratoga marked a turning point in the war. It showed the rest of the world that the United States might actually succeed in winning its independence from Britain.

News of this victory reached King Louis XVI in France in December 1777, and France agreed to recognize American independence. France declared war on Britain and promised to supply the United States with money, equipment, and thousands of troops.

This aid took many months to arrive. Meanwhile, Washington and his men were suffering a bitter winter at Valley Forge, Pennsylvania. The men lived in tents or windowless huts, sleeping on wooden bunks or straw mats. Many had no clothes except rags, and most were weak from disease or starvation.

During 1777–1778, the American army spent a miserable winter at Valley Forge, Pennsylvania (near Philadelphia). Since the farmers sold their food to the British troops for more money, the men had little to eat. Mostly they ate flour and water mixed together and cooked on hot stones. The soldiers called this food "firecakes."

AMERICAN INDEPENDENCE

Although the war would last another four years, France's entry into the struggle guaranteed an American victory. In August 1781, Washington marched his troops south from New York to Yorktown, Virginia, where, supported by the French navy, they bombarded the British into surrendering. The war was finally over. The American colonies no longer belonged to Britain. They were a new country.

When Lord Cornwallis was surrounded at Yorktown, one of his last efforts at counterattack was to try to infect the approaching French and American troops with smallpox. He officially surrendered to General Washington on October 19, 1781, marking the end of the Revolutionary War.

George Washington resigned as the commander-in-chief of the United States army on December 19, 1783. He was 51 years old and he wanted to go home to his family. It was time for the new country to move forward.

But there were still challenges ahead. The Articles of Confederation were established on March 1, 1781. In them, the 13 British colonies officially became the United States of America.

However, there was no single authority set up to settle any conflict that might arise between the states. Nor was there any mention of taxes that would be necessary, or how the new nation would manage its troops for defense and protection. Something more had to be done. The United States of America could possibly fall apart.

In the summer of 1787, 55 delegates from the different states came once again to Philadelphia to solve the country's problems at the Constitutional Convention. They created the Constitution, the rules that govern the United States of America. The Constitution described how the country would be organized and governed, with an elected president and a legislature, called Congress. Now it was time to elect the first president of the United States.

George Washington was chosen as one of Virginia's five delegates to the Constitutional Convention. He then presided over the convention for the next four months, speaking very little but maintaining a strong presence and a firm position on matters of the Constitution.

WASHINGTON'S PRESIDENCY

In early 1789, the states held elections to select members of the new government. When the presidential votes were cast, George Washington was elected unanimously as the first president of the United States. There were no political parties, and no presidential campaigns. As the new president, he got a salary of $25,000 per year.

Washington was reluctant to be president. He did not trust his abilities and feared his motives would be criticized as he tried to lead the new government. But this did not worry the American people.

One of the first actions that Washington took was to push the adoption of the Bill of Rights (the first 10 amendments to the Constitution). The Constitution was established to organize the government, but it said little about the rights of the people. The Bill of Rights secured the people's rights as part of the Constitution in 1791. Washington worked hard at getting the new government started and served as an example for the future presidents to follow.

After four years as president, Washington was easily elected to a second term in office. During his second term, people disagreed about how the country should be run. Slowly, these people formed political parties. The Federalists held the belief that the central government should be strong and powerful. The Democratic-Republicans believed that the rights of the people were the most important. Washington tried to stay neutral and balance their interests. He thought both were important. But he tended to agree with the Federalists more often.

THE BILL OF RIGHTS

The Bill of Rights was added to the United States Constitution in 1791. It outlined the rights of the people, including:

Freedom of religion

Freedom of speech

The right to a trial by jury

THE FEDERAL CITY

After his inauguration, Washington and his new government met in New York City. In 1790 the government moved to Philadelphia, the second-largest city in the new country. The government did not move to Washington, D.C. until 1800. George and Martha never lived in the White House.

Philadelphia, in 1790, when it served as the temporary home of the federal government. The debate of where the capital should be located threatened the unity of the new United States. Each state wanted it to be within its borders.

Washington, D.C., the new federal city, was planned by the French architect Pierre L'Enfant in 1791. Congress approved the land on the Potomac River in 1790. Both the land and the architect were picked by George Washington.

When Washington became president, there was no capital for the central (or federal) government. Washington agreed with the idea that there should be a special "federal city" where the United States government would be located. He chose 10 square miles of land near the center of the 13 states to become Washington, D.C. This city near Mount Vernon became the capital district of the entire United States. The land for the new city was donated by Virginia and Maryland.

Washington approved the plans for the new city and saw it being built. Always a modest man, he never called it "Washington, D.C." He always called it the "federal city."

WASHINGTON'S LEGACY

George Washington was such an important figure in the shaping of the United States that it is hard to pick out his one contribution that stands out from the others. He spent much of his life in service to his country. Serving in the army, he led the United States forces to victory. Without this feat, the United States would not have become the country it is today.

George Washington authorized the building of the Capitol of the United States government in 1793. It took 34 years, six presidents, and six different architects to finish this building. Congress began using the building in 1800.

Tribute to Washington

George Washington was "...first in war, first in peace, and first in the hearts of his countrymen."

General Henry Lee, at Washington's funeral

He then approached his presidency with the same dedication and careful judgment as his military service. He firmly believed and insisted on a national strength, dignity, and identity. One final noteworthy example of his character was his decision not to accept a third term as president. He felt it was time for the country to elect a new chief executive. In 1796 the United States elected John Adams. The government changed hands without having to fight a war. This was an important first example of democracy in action.

Washington was 65 years old when he retired to Mount Vernon, but he did not enjoy his retirement for long. One day after going riding in the wintry rain, he was stricken with a very bad case of tonsillitis. He died on December 14, 1799, at the age of 67.

There are many memorials to George Washington throughout the United States. This statue is in the public gardens in Boston, Massachusetts.

TIMELINE

1732–George Washington is born in Virginia (February 22)

1748–George gets his first big surveying job

1752–Lawrence Washington (George's brother) dies; George takes over his military assignment

1753–George Washington goes to the Ohio Territory with Governor Dinwiddie's message to the French

1754–George Washington leads troops to the Ohio Territory, and the French and Indian War starts

1755–George Washington becomes commander of the Virginia militia

1758–George Washington leaves the military

1759–George Washington marries Martha Dandridge Custis on January 6

1775–George Washington attends the Second Continental Congress as a delegate from Virginia and is elected commander-in-chief of the American troops

1776–The Declaration of Independence is signed; Washington's troops cross the Delaware River

1777–American victory at Saratoga; freezing winter in Valley Forge

1778–France and the United States sign a treaty for French aid

1781–The British army surrenders to George Washington

1783–George Washington resigns from the army

1787–George Washington is president of the Constitutional Convention

1789–George Washington is elected first president of the United States

1792–George Washington is elected to a second term as president

1793–Begins to build the new Federal City (Washington, D.C.)

1796–George Washington retires; John Adams is elected president

1799–George Washington dies (December 14)

GLOSSARY

Colony (KOL-uh-nee) An area of land ruled by another (parent) country

Delegate (DEL-uh-guht) A person chosen to act for others; a representative

Frontier (fruhn-TIHR) An area that is on the edge of settled territory, right next to the wilderness

Government (GUHV-urn-muhnt) The rules, organizations, and people that run the country

Inauguration (in-aw-gyuh-RAY-shuhn) The ceremony that takes place when a new president begins his or her job

Legislature (LEJ-iss-lay-chur) A group of delegates that gather to make laws for their land

Militia (muh-LISH-uh) A group of people who form their own local military service

Neutral (NOO-truhl) Not taking either side in a disagreement

Rebel (REB-uhl) A person who disagrees with his ruler or government

Survey (SUR-vay) To map and measure a piece of land

Widow (WID-oh) A woman whose husband has died

FURTHER READING AND INFORMATION

Books to Read

Gross, Ruth Belov. *If You Grew Up With George Washington*. New York: Scholastic Trade, 1993.

Marrin, Albert. *George Washington & the Founding of a Nation*. New York: Dutton Children's Books, 2001.

Old, Wendie C. *George Washington. (United States Presidents)*.Springfield, N.J.: Enslow, 1997.

Simon, Charnon. *Martha Dandridge Custis Washington: 1731-1802*. New York: Children's Press, 2000.

Weber, Michael. *Washington, Adams, and Jefferson. (Complete History of our Presidents, v. 1)*. Vero Beach, Fla.: Rourke Corp., 1997.

Videos

The American Experience: George Washington—The Man Who Wouldn't Be King. WGBH Boston Video, 1997.

Biography—George Washington: American Revolutionary. A&E Entertainment, 2001.

Biography—George Washington: Founding Father. A&E Entertainment, 1995.

George Washington: The Forging of a Nation. MGM Studios, 1986.

George Washington: The Unknown Years. Acorn Media, 1997.

The Story of George Washington. Robert Quakenbush Studios, 1989.

INDEX